CW00762362

Songs From Leinster

SONGS FROM LEINSTER

BY W. M. LETTS

AUTHOR OF

"A ROUGH WAY" AND "DIANA DETHRONED"

LONDON

JOHN MURRAY, ALBEMARLE STREET, W.

1920

FIRST EDITION (Smith, Elder & Co.)   *May*, 1913

Reprinted   .   .   .   .   .   *December*, 1913

Reprinted   .   .   .   .   .   *July*, 1914

Reprinted (John Murray)   .   .   .   *September*, 1917

Reprinted   .   .   .   .   .   *January*, 1920

CONTENTS

IN A WEXFORD VILLAGE

IN DUBLIN

CONTENTS

A FIRE OF TURF

SONGS IN THREE COUNTIES

CONTENTS

These songs have appeared for the most part in the *Spectator* and *Westminster Gazette*, others in the *Saturday Review*, *Nation*, *Cornhill*, and the *Odd Volume*.

IN A WEXFORD VILLAGE

THE HARBOUR

I THINK if I lay dying in some land
  Where Ireland is no more than just a name,
My soul would travel back to find that strand
  From whence it came.

I'd see the harbour in the evening light,
  The old men staring at some distant ship,
The fishing-boats they fasten left and right
  Beside the slip.

The sea-wrack lying on the wind-swept shore,
  The grey thorn bushes growing in the sand
Our Wexford coast from Arklow to Cahore—
  My native land.

The little houses climbing up the hill,
  Sea daisies growing in the sandy grass,

3   B 2

The tethered goats that wait large-eyed and still
   To watch you pass.

The women at the well with dripping pails,
   Their men colloguing by the harbour wall,
The coils of rope, the nets, the old brown sails,
   I'd know them all.

And then the Angelus—I'd surely see
   The swaying bell against a golden sky,
So God, Who kept the love of home in me,
   Would let me die.

STORM

THERE's a storm is blowing up from the sea
(That Christ in mercy may save us all),
For the waves are lepping the harbour wall,
An' dirty weather it's sure to be.
The storm dog shone in the morning sky,
And the waves to the west are ten foot high.
God in Heaven! the waves are white—
Let You watch near the boats to-night!

For it's sure enough when the shadows fall
Sorrow will come for some of us here,
In the cold black night and its cold black fear:
Fear of the sea and fear of the squall.
A woeful thing it is to be wed
To a man who looks to the sea for bread!
Holy Mary, pity our plight,
Let you pray for our men to-night!

There's Patrick is in it and Christy too,
A soft young lad, an' he not sixteen—
An' his brother drownded last Hallow E'en.
God help his mother, what will she do ?
She had a right to have bid him stay,
But the young lads fret till they go away.
God keep Christy and John in sight,
Save them both from their death to-night !

There is Daniel Connor and young Tom Byrne,
With a child at home not three days old ;
But it's hungry the child will be and cold,
If there's no man in it, nor wage to earn ;
An' lonesome herself will be this day
That's sick and weak, an' her man away.
Heart of Heaven, pity her fright,
Send her comfort this long black night !

The wind of the world is lashing the sea,
The waves lep high like men at a fair,
Wicked old men with their silvery hair.
Sorrow and weeping for some one there'll be,

STORM

Toil for the men, an' danger and fear,
With the cold black death that is waiting near.
God Almighty, pity their plight,
Let Christ walk on the waves to-night.

THE OLD WEXFORD WOMAN

WHAT do I think of the women that's in it?
    'Tis little enough ;
If you offered them flax would they throuble to spin it?
Faith ! I've a notion before they'd begin it
    You'd wait for your stuff.

Would they pick wool from the hedges and ditches?
    We did in my day.
But it's easier plans they have now to make riches :
Why would you sew when machines makes your
    stitches?
    Sure, that's what they say.

'Tis truth I'd no hand for making a letter,
    But where was the lack?
An' I couldn't read books any more than that setter.
But for baking or stitching there wasn't a better,
    Or making a brack.

8

The black fasts were kept without hesitation,
    I tell you no lie.
Arrah! now there's no manner of strength in the
    nation,
It's sorra a one but needs dispensation
    For fear they would die.

The way they are now they're seeking their pleasure,
    The days are too slow.
They'd look twice at a spade were they hunting for
    treasure,
It's towns that they want, and evenings of leisure
    To street to and fro.

What is it they're afther there in the city
    That takes them away?
It's new clothes they'll be buying to make themselves
    pretty;
No value at all—an' sure that's a pity.
    They'll know it some day.

What do I think of the race that we're rarin'?
    They're not worth my shawl.

For it's sooner they're threadbare an' nobody
    carin'.
Mine was the days—but there's no good com-
    parin'.
    God help us all.

DROWNDED

Tom Cassidy is drownded—
That God may keep his soul.
His body floats in the deep cold sea,
An' only the herring and mackerel shoal
　　Can tell where Tom may be.
　　May Christ have pity on his soul,—
　　An' that He'll pity me.

Tom threatened that he'd bring me
Strange shells from foreign sands,
An' Chiney silk that would make a gown,
With three ostrich feathers from foreign lands
　　All creamy white and brown.
　　My grief!   I stand with empty hands,
　　An' him and all gone down.

There's none can ever tell me
How long he may have striven

With the cold black waves that choked his life,
An' him with the sins on his soul unshriven,
  In that his mortal strife.
  God's mercy on the unforgiven,
  And me his promised wife.

  My curse upon the ocean,
  My curse upon the wind !
That's taken my heart's bright core on me,
An' made him a sepulchre none can find
  But them that's in the sea.
  Why would they leave the old behind
  And take the young and free ?

IN SERVICE

LITTLE Nellie Cassidy has got a place in town,
    She wears a fine white apron,
    She wears a new black gown.
An' the quarest little cap at all with straymers hang-
    ing down.

I met her one fine evening stravagin' down the street,
    A feathered hat upon her head,
    And boots upon her feet.
"Now, Mick," says she, "may God be praised that
    you and I should meet.

"It's lonesome in the city with such a crowd," say
    she ;
    " I'm lost without the bog-land,
    I'm lost without the sea,
An' the harbour an' the fishing-boats that sail out
    fine and free.

"I'd give a golden guinea to stand upon the shore,
　　To see the big waves lepping,
　　To hear them splash and roar,
To smell the tar and the drying nets, I'd not be
　asking more.

"To see the small white houses, their faces to the
　sea,
　　The childher in the doorway,
　　Or round my mother's knee ;
For I'm strange and lonesome missing them, God
　keep them all," says she.

Little Nellie Cassidy earns fourteen pounds and
　more,
　　Waiting on the quality,
　　And answering the door—
But her heart is some place far away upon the
　Wexford shore.

GRANDEUR

Poor Mary Byrne is dead,
  . An' all the world may see
Where she lies upon her bed
  Just as fine as quality.

She lies there still and white,
  With candles either hand
That'll guard her through the night
  Sure she never was so grand.

She holds her rosary,
  Her hands clasped on her breast.
Just as dacint as can be
  In the habit she's been dressed.

In life her hands were red
  With every sort of toil,
But they're white now she is dead,
  An' they've sorra mark of soil.

15

The neighbours come and go,
　　They kneel to say a prayer.
I wish herself could know
　　Of the way she's lyin' there.

It was work from morn till night,
　　And hard she earned her bread :
But I'm thinking she's a right
　　To be aisy now she's dead.

When other girls were gay,
　　At wedding or at fair,
She'd be toiling all the day,
　　Not a minyit could she spare.

An' no one missed her face,
　　Or sought her in a crowd,
But to-day they throng the place
　　Just to see her in her shroud.

The creature in her life
　　Drew trouble with each breath ,
She was just " poor Jim Byrne's wife "—
　　But she's lovely in her death.

16

GRANDEUR

I wish the dead could see
  The splendour of a wake,
For it's proud herself would be
  Of the keening that they make.

Och! little Mary Byrne,
  You welcome every guest,
Is it now you take your turn
  To be merry with the rest?

I'm thinking you'd be glad,
  Though the angels make your bed,
Could you see the care we've had
  To respect you—now you're dead.

THE CHOICE

Saint Joseph, let you send me a comrade true and
    kind,
For the one I'm after seeking, it beats the world to
    find.

There's Christy Shee's a decent lad, but he's too lank
    and tall;
And Shaneen Burke will never do, for he's a foot
    too small.

John Heffernan has gold enough, but sure he'd have
    me bet
With talkin' of the wife that died a year before
    we met.

Young Pat Delaney suits my mind, but he's a thrifle
    wild;
And Tim I've known too well itself from since I was a
    child.

THE CHOICE

Old Dennis Morrissey has pigs, and cattle in the
    byre,
But, someways, I don't fancy him the far side o' the
    fire.

I'd have Saint Joseph choose me a comrade rich and
    kind —
And if it's Terry Sullivan—maybe I mightn't mind.

A SERMON

THE fish have left the coast a while ago,
Bad luck it is that's in it, faith ! that's so,
  For there's little you can win
  When you'll scarcely see a fin,
An' when food is dear to buy and wages low.

Tis what his Reverence says to us this day ·
" Need yous wonder that the fish are gone away ?
  'Twas the sights they saw on shore
  That had scared them more and more,
And so, hadn't they a right to swim away ?

" 'Twas the couples that were gaming on the sands,
'Linking arms they were, maybe, or squeezin' hands,
  Now, there's not a herring sprat
  That could stand the like o' that—
So they're seeking for more Christianable lands.

A SERMON

"But let yous mend your manners now," says he,
"Let the lads all walk together decently,
    Let the girls not be so bold,
    An' maybe, before you're old,
The fish will thravel back across the sea."

BLESSING

At night I sit beside the hearth,
  And watch the glowing sod;
I tell my beads and say a name
  That's known to me and God.

That's surely known to me and God,
  For every night and day
I call a blessing on the one
  That travels far away.

That travels far away itself
  To earn a stranger's gold
May God's love be a mantle now
  To shield him from the cold;

To shield him from the bitter cold,
  And from a bitter tongue;
It's harsh and strange are foreign lands
  To one that's soft and young.

BLESSING

To one whose heart is hot and young,
    The thought of home is dear,
O Heart of Christ, shield him I love,
    And hold him warm and near.

Hold him that travels warm and near,
    And keep his spirit white ;
Be safety to him through the day,
    And shelter through the night.

Be shelter through the long, dark night,
    Wherever he may be.
Send thoughts of Ireland to his dreams,
    And keep him true to me.

HALLOWS' E'EN

THE girls are laughing with the boys, and gaming
    by the fire,
They're wishful, every one of them to see her
    heart's desire.
'Twas Thesie cut the barnbrack and found the ring
    inside,
Before next Hallows' E'en has dawned herself will be
    a bride.
But little Mollie stands alone outside the cabin
    door,
And breaks her heart for one the waves threw dead
    upon the shore.

'Twas Katie's nut lepped from the hearth, and left
    poor Pat's alone,
But Ellen's stayed by Christy Byrne's upon the wide
    hearthstone.
An' all the while the childher bobbed for apples set
    afloat,

The old men smoked their pipes and talked about the
foundered boat.
But Mollie walked upon the cliff, and never feared
the rain ;
She called the name of one she loved and bid him
come again.

Young Peter pulled the cabbage-stump to win a
wealthy wife,
Rosanna threw the apple-peel to know who'd share
her life ;
And Lizzie had a looking-glass she'd hid in some
dark place
To try if there, foreninst her own, she'd see her
comrade's face.
But Mollie walked along the quay where Terry's feet
had trod,
And sobbed her grief out in the night, with no one
near but God.

She heard the laughter from the house, she heard the
fiddle played ;
She called her dead love to her side—why would she
be afraid ?

She took his cold hands in her own, she had no thought
of dread,

And not a star looked out to watch the living kiss
the dead.

.   .   .   .   .   .

The lads are gaming with the girls, and laughing by
the fire.

But Mollie, in the cold, dark night, has found her
heart's desire.

DAN O'SHEE

If I could fetch the moon down from the sky,
    I'd give her for a lamp to Dan O'Shee;
So he'd never fear the darkness of the night,
    Or the depth o' dark upon the winter sea.

If every beech leaf in the wood were gold,
    I'd gather gold all day and never tire.
It's sorra care should come the winter long,
    With the turf stack full and cattle in the byre.

If I should win the keys of Heaven's gates,
    And find them open wide to welcome me,
I'd ask of God to bid them wait awhile,
    Till I'd enter side by side with Dan O'Shee.

IN DUBLIN

THE TOWN

I wonder now does God look down
    Upon the town,
And what He's thinking when He sees
The people swarming there like bees,
The alleys and the dirty lanes,
The moidher of the trams and trains;
The stately carriages galore,
    And then the poor,
Who traipis in the bitter sleet,
With broken boots upon their feet.
I wonder what He thinks at night,
When angels set the stars alight,
And in the town the lamps are bright.
Does He watch gaming rascals cheat,
Old drunken villyains curse and fight,
While girls, grown shameless, walk the street?

Always God hears the Cherubim
    Sing praise to Him.

But where He's sitting on His throne
Can He hear starving women moan?
Above the harping of each saint
Are little childher's voices faint?
Can He in all the music hear
 Them sob for fear?
On dirty pavements babies sprawl,
With them to mind them scarce less small.
It's sure God hears the cries of these,
And all the oaths and blasphemies
Of thim that's never on their knees.
He hears the drunkards shout and bawl
Above the angels' melodies—
I wonder what God thinks at all?

IN THE STREET

I'VE seen a woman kneeling down
    In the dirty street.
An' she took no heed of her tattered gown,
    Or the broken boots on her feet;
An' she took no heed of the people there,
Rich and poor that would stand and stare
    At a woman kneeling in prayer
      In the street.

    For the thing that she spied
At the back of the great shop window pane
Was a cross with a Figure crucified
She took no heed of the driving rain,
    An' thim that would turn to look again;
She took no heed of the noisy street,
    But knelt down there at her Saviour's feet.
What matter at all what the place might be?
To one poor soul it was Calvary.

QUANTITY AND QUALITY

THE poor have childher and to spare,
But with the quality they're rare,
Where money's scarce the childher's many,
Where money's thick you'll scarce find any.
Some wanted here, too many there—
        It's quare.

Now, if the rich and poor could share,
There'd soon be childher everywhere;
But God have pity on the mother
That gives her child up to another;
An' so you'll find a mansion bare,
A cabin rich in all that's fair—
        It's quare.

MIND YOURSELF

" Just mind yourself," says he to me,
" Avoid the divil's company.
The wage he gives won't make yous fat,
A greasy coat, a broken hat,
An' trousers patched at either knee.

" A man who drives a car needs be
Aware to mind he's not too free,
But sober as a cardinal's cat—
    Just mind yourself."

" Avoid them treating lads," says he,
" An' join the men's Sodality.
Don't cock your little finger, Pat,
There's ruin in the like o' that,
And riches in sobriety—
    Just mind yourself."

To mind oneself. To avoid drinking too freely
Cock the little finger. The action of a man holding a glass to his lips.

THE CRIB

IN THE CARMELITE CHURCH, DUBLIN

Foreninst the Crib there kneels a little child,
Behind him in her ragged shawl his mother,
For all the ages that have passed one child
　　Still finds God in another.

Now, look-a how he wonders when he sees
The shepherds with their lambs beside the manger,
The cattle, poor dumb creatures, looking down
　　Upon the little Stranger.

An' there's our Saviour lying in the hay,
Behind Him in her shawl His watchful mother;
Two mothers with their sons, each knows the joys
　　And sorrows of the other.

The father kneels away there by the door,
The hands he clasps in prayer are rough with labour;

Outside the Church the people travel by,
The sick and sad, the needy, the neglected.
But just across the threshold Bethlehem lies,
Where none will be rejected.

THE BOLD UNBIDDABLE CHILD

Now what is he after below in the street?
  (God save us, he's terrible wild!)
Is it stirrin' the gutter around with his feet?
He'd best be aware when the two of us meet.
        Come in out o' that,
        Come in,
        You bold unbiddable child!

He's after upsetting the Widow Foy's pail—
  She'll murder him yet, Widow Foy!
An' he's pulling the massacree dog by the tail,
By the hokey! that young one is born for the gaol.
        Come in out o' that,
        Come in,
        You rogue of a villyainous boy!

Go tell him his mother is seeking a stick
  For a boy that is terrible wild.

If he cares for his feelings he'd better be quick,
Och! he'll draw in his horns when he sees me, will
 Mick.
  Come in out o' that,
  Come in,
  You bold unbiddable child!

FOR SIXPENCE

In the old days when the pit seats at the Abbey Theatre Dublin, cost sixpence at matinées.

For sixpence I have been to Tir-na-n-oge
    (No more I had to pay)
And looked my fill at kings and gods and fools—
    May God be with the day.

For sixpence I have seen the heart of mirth
    And sorrow's stricken face;
Have laughed aloud and dried my covert tears
    Before I left my place.

For sixpence I have left the world outside
    Rainswept and chill and mean,
And been a guest in Emain Macha's halls.
    Companion to a queen.

FOR SIXPENCE

And all for sixpence I have heard fine talk
From playboys, rogues and tramps,
And so forgot the east wind in the streets,
The fog, the dim-eyed lamps.

Sixpence the passport to this splendid world
Enchanted, sad or gay.
And you the playboy of them all I saw
For sixpence — William Fay.

SYNGE'S GRAVE

My grief! that they have laid you in the town
Within the moidher of its thousand wheels
And busy feet that travel up and down.

They had a right to choose a better bed
Far off among the hills where silence steals
In on the soul with comfort-bringing tread.

The curlew would have keened for you all day,
The wind across the heather cried Ochone
For sorrow of his brother gone away.

In Glenmalure, far off from town-born men,
Why would they not have let you sleep alone
At peace there in the shadow of the glen?

To tend your grave you should have had the sun,
The fraughan and the moss, the heather brown
And goise turned gold for joy of Spring begun.

SYNGE'S GRAVE

You should have had your brothers, wind and rain,
And in the dark the stars all looking down
To ask, " When will he take the road again ? "

The herdsmen of the lone back hills, that drive
The mountain ewes to some far distant Fair,
Would stand and say, " We knew him well alive.

That God may rest his soul!" Then they would
    pass
Into the silence brooding everywhere,
And leave you to your sleep below the grass.

But now among these alien city graves,
What way are you without the rough wind's breath
You free-born son of mountains and wild waves?

Ah! God knows better—here you've no abode,
So long ago you had the laugh at death,
And rose and took the windswept mountain road.

ANGELS UNAWARES

She minds the childher all the day,
  A baby tucked inside her shawl;
Faulting the young ones when they stray
  Along the street beyond her call.

Her mother has not time to spare
  For sittin' under chick or child,
So Katey has the lot to care,
  The lads to keep from running wild.

The sense comes soon to thim that's poor,
  Herself could scarcely walk when she
Made room for younger ones galore,
  And rocked the baby on her knee.

Barefooted, with her share of dirt,
  But steadfast for her years is Kate;
The likes of her don't come to hurt,
  Though sure she's only rising eight.

44

You'll meet her streeling through the rain,
  The baby sleeping on her breast,
Or by some big shop window pane
  Lookin' how quality is dressed.

Happy as little kings they stand,
  Staring at cakes or sweets or toys ;
She has a sister by the hand,
  Her skirts are clutched by two small boys.

Their faces pressed against the glass.
  They do be lettin' on to choose
The best of everything they pass,
  Toy soldiers, dolls, or scarlet shoes.

Then through the chapel door they streel
  When Katey bids to say a prayer ;
Hand clasped in hand the young ones kneel
  To beg God have them in His care.

   .   .   .   .   .

There's other girls in this same street
  As careless as the breeze of June ;
They do be dancing on their feet
  The time the organ plays a tune.

A skipping rope is their delight,
   The lamp-post serves them for a swing,
You'll say that Katey has a right
   To jump with them and dance and sing.

You think her life is hard, may-be?
   You'd have her playing bat and ball?
But sure the best of games, says she,
   Is playing mother to them all.

THREE SLUM PORTRAITS

I

FROM A WINDOW

("The Retort Courteous")

She leans out of her window an' says she,
  "You're growing woeful stout itself of late,
  I'd soon jump over you as round you, Kate,"
With that she laughs and throws a wink at me.

'Twas some old one she faulted down below.
  "I heerd," she says, "they borrowed your two feet
  The time they wanted flag-stones for the street,
I thought I'd ask yourself now was it so?"

"It's quare," says she, "you'll get a shoe that size,
  They'll have your likeness on the paper soon,
  A foot that bet the 29th o' June." *
She looked at me with her two laughing eyes.

* St. Peter and St. Paul.

47

She listens for a minyit—then says she,
  " For all the six-foot polis in the place,
  Next time we meet I'll bang that off your face,
You'll learn to know your betters so, maybe."

No more she says but " Thank you for that same."
  So steps across the room with hasty tread,
  And from the dresser picks a fish's head,
Then leans out of her window and takes aim.

II

GOD'S IMAGE

MADE in God's image ? Look at where he stands
   Above there at the corner of the street
   The poor old porter-shark daren't trust his feet,
An' so he grabs the lamp post with both hands.
Who'd think we live in Christianable lands ?
   He's one o' thim old murdering roughs you'll meet
   Stravagin' with their baskets through the sleet.
They're after picking cockles on the sands.

The dogs, poor dacint creatures, daren't come nigh,
   Thim with drink taken arn't so soft or kind.
So he stands swaying, bawling to the sky
   Like some old omadhaun that's lost his mind
Made in God's image ? Watch him stagger by—
   God's likeness there is mortal hard to find.

III

LITTLE PETER MORRISSEY

Poor little Peter Morrissey, what way is he at all?
His mother's supping porter till she's like to get a
    fall,
And all the work his father does is propping up a
    wall.

He's ne'er a shirt upon his back, nor ganzy * to his
    name,
There never was a pair of boots the likes of him
    could claim,
An' he's after treading on some glass the way he's
    walking lame.

When decent childher lie in bed you'll see him out at
    night,

* "Ganzy"—a vest or jersey.

50

Where he's screeching " Mail " and " Herald," or
    joining in a fight
To hold his own with other lads, an' he not half their
    height.

You'll see him in the winter time stravagin' through
    the wet ;
He's not so wishful to go home where likely he'll be
    bet ;
An' if he's kilt with cold an' damp, who is there that
    will fret ?

Poor little Peter Morrissey, his troubles have begun,
And yet I've often seen himself sit laughing in the
    sun,
And he's always ready after school to sing and lep
    and run.

His mother likes the drink too well to spare the
    child a toy,
You'd think, maybe, the way he is was far enough
    from joy,
And yet—there's time I envy him the light heart of
    a boy.

CHRISTMAS IN THE WORKHOUSE

Iт's Christmas Eve they tell me, but in the Work-
house ward
One day is like another an' both is mortal long.
What sort of grand rejoicings could the like of us
afford,
That's poor old pauper women who could never
raise a song?
Peace and good will the angels sing
To Christianable people.
You'll hear the merry bells ring out
From every Dublin steeple.

There's paper decorations to hang upon the wall,
And scrubbin' and conthrivin'——themselves is fearful clane.
They're lettin' on it's Christmas Eve, but troth! I'd
quit it all
To walk the dirty world outside and see the street
again.

Peace and good will the angels sing
To every living sinner.
(On Christmas Day the Guardians give
Plum pudding for our dinner.)

The ould one that's beside me she coughs with every
breath,
The one beyant, the villyain, her temper's fearful
short ;
But it's in this place we're gathered, an' like to be
till death,
Amn't I praying every minyit to love them as
I ought ?
Peace and good will the angels sing,
And let you love your brother ;
But angels in a Workhouse ward
Would maybe hate each other.

A tidy-living person I was when I was young,
As tidy-living person as ever walked in shoes.
But it's quare and bad ch'racters I've got to live
among,
Wid some that's in it never had ch'racters they
could lose.

53

Peace and good will the angels sing,
   But here's a world of sorrow.
(Och, glory be ! ourselves will dine
   On rale roast beef to-morrow.)

THE LITTLE CHILDHER IN THE STREET

THE little childher in the street—
   It's shipwrecked sure they are with cold,
   There's some of them not eight years old,
And ne'er a boot upon their feet.
To beg a copper they go far
   In rain and frost, in snow and sleet.
   The little childher in the street,
You'd pity them the way they are.

There's other childher warmly clad,
   That live in houses in the square,
   They all have coppers and to spare,
The sight of them would make you glad;
A nurse, be sure, is never far
   To shield them from the rain and cold.
   They're guarded like a bag of gold—
You'd envy them the way they are.

Now them that look so rich and grand,
   And them that shiver in the street,
   I wonder will they ever meet
And walk together hand in hand.
I do be thinking when they're small
   It's like they are as peas in pod ;
   Maybe they're like as that to God—
It's sure enough He made them all.

A FIRE OF TURF

A FIRE OF TURF

In summer time I foot the turf
And lay the sods to dry,
South wind and lark's song, and the sun far up in
the sky.
I pile them on the turf stack
Against the time of snow,
Black frost, a gale from the north, who minds what
winds will blow?

Now winter's here, make up the fire,
And let you bolt the door.
A wind across the mountains, a draught across the
floor,
I'll not be heeding cold or rain,
Or moaning of the wind,
With the turf fire, the hearth stone, the notions in
my mind.

I've seen a power of years itself
That's gone beyond recall,
The leaves of spring, the days of youth, where are
they now at all ?
The withered leaves lie in the glen,
The days of youth are dead,
Now it's long nights and long thoughts while the
sods o' turf glow red.

I see myself a barefoot child,
I see myself a lad,
When the gold upon the gorse bush was all the gold
I had.
I do be having fine old dreams
Of days were long ago,
When the wind keens, the night falls, and the embers
glow.

THE OLD MAN REMEMBERS:—

THE CHAPEL ON THE HILL

THE Chapel of my childhood
  Is on the green hillside,
And in the long grass up the hill
  The graves of them that's died.

My mother often took me
  When I was young and small,
I'd kneel upon her skirt and count
  The Stations on the wall.

Each evening in the Maytime
  The Rosary we'd say;
You'd hear beyant the Chapel wall
  The corncrakes in the hay.

The flowers round the altar,
  They made the air smell sweet,

And cool the Chapel floor would be
  To little childher's feet.

It's scarce a day was passing
  But there I'd be awhile ;
I mind the way the boys' bare feet
  Went patting up the aisle.

The girls would come from lessons,
  And kneel to say a prayer,
You'd see the noonday sunshine caught
  In Mary Connor's hair.

VOICES

Oh, Cuckoo, Cuckoo away on Knockree,
'Tis well for yourself now you're idle and free,
For there you are gaming away on the hill,
And I in the schoolhouse obliged to sit still.

  Is it " When will you come ? "
  When I finish my sum.
  If the clock would strike four
  Then they'll open the door.

Let you call me then, Cuckoo, call loud and I'll
 come.

Away in the meadow the corncrakes shout
" Will you come now an' seek me ? Come out, come
 out.
I'm under the window, I'm close to the wall,
I'm holding the world up for fear it would fall. *

  Am I under your feet,
  Or away in the wheat ?

 * According to a country legend related by Mr. Padraic Colum
the corncrake lies on his back crying, " I hold the world. '

Let you seek for me soon ;
I've been calling since noon."
And it's here I sit working, nigh kilt with the heat.

The king has a right to make it a rule
That only old men should be sitting in school.
I'm moidhered with voices singing and humming,
" The hours are passing and when are you coming ? "
    Just a minyit or more
    An' they'll open the door.
    When I've finished my sum
    Be aware ! for I'll come.
Ah ! Now glory to goodness ! the clock's striking
    four !

THE FAIR

Oh ! we're off to the Fair now the lot of us together,
The yellow sunlight everywhere—sure that's the
lovely weather !
And amn't I six foot high to-day with pride and joy
of heart,
The way I'm driving to the Fair in a fine new ass-
and-cart ?

The pigs are screeching merrily at all the jolts and
lurches,
The wonder of the world we are from here until the
Churches ;
The speckly hen, poor decent bird, has lost her wits
with scare,
It's well you'd know the noise she makes that we're
going to the Fair.

65   F

The quality will stare when they see the way we're
    driving,

The polis stand in wonderment to watch the cart
    arriving ;

And the people that's stravagin' about the market
    square

Will be kilt with envy when ourselves come driving
    to the Fair.

But the best time of all is the time the evening
    closes,

With a wind blowing from the south is sweet with
    wild hedge roses.

And we're counting out our money and proud and
    glad of heart

The way we're driving home again in our fine new
    ass-and-cart.

QUESTIONS

I asked old Dan the fiddler if he could tell me true
What lies beyond the mountains that rise so dim an'
    blue.
I asked him if the sun would sleep among the hills at
    night
The time you see Tibradden dark against the golden
    light?

I asked him did the leprechaun hide there his pot of
    gold,
An' people reach a hundred and no one think them
    old;
And was it truth the rabbits there could talk if
    they'd a mind;
The cows be Christianable beasts, the goats all soft
    and kind?

I asked him was it true at all the fruit trees there
    grew wild
With pears and plums and apples to give to any
    child ;
And had he seen the fairy farms, the weeshy sheep
    live there,
The tiny pigs all black an' white, the chuckins small
    and quare ?

Old Dan the fiddler answered, " The place is there to
    find,
But what way would I see it an' I so nearly blind?
I've travelled all the mountain roads, the bogs where
    curlews cry.
I've heard the heather whisper as I was passing by.

" There's things that's plain to childher the likes of
    us can't see,
It's when you're old you call it dreams, an' that's the
    way," says he.
We parted at the cross roads, he laughed did quare
    old Dan—
But I'll climb the mountains surely, the time I'm
    grown a man.

COWSLIP TIME

God bless the time when cowslips grow
High and low, high and low ;
When never a place you're like to pass,
But there's cowslips deep in the meadow grass ;
Over the rath when the winds do blow
They're swinging and nodding to and fro,
Oh ! it's well to be young when the cowslips grow !

Old age will come—what matter so ?
High and low, high and low
The cowslips shine when the spring comes round,
In every meadow and patch of ground.
And you'll watch your childher's childher go
Off to the fields where the spring winds blow.
Oh ! it's well for the world when the cowslips grow !

SCARED

THESE dusky evenings in December
  I do be scared with sudden fright,
So many things you'd disremember
  Shows quare an' darkish in the night.
    Sure kilt you'd be if a dog should bark,
    Or an old cow wheeze in the lonesome dark ;
    For who can tell who's in it at all,
    With the Tax man murdered there by the wall
    An' the druidy stone foreninst the wood,
    Where you'd maybe see what isn't good.
    An' the haunted house—Och ! glory be,
    There's a power of terrible things you'd see
      In the dark.

I'm feared itself lest some black stranger
  Would step behind me on the grass ;
Or goodness knows what sudden danger
  Might lep upon me as I pass.

For strange an' lonesome the roads do seem
Like a far-off place you'd see in a dream ;
An' you'd never know who you'd meet at the
    turn,
Old crazy Nelly or mad John Byrne,
Or the headless one that wrings her hands,
Where the old deserted cabin stands,
Or the fairy dog. Och ! glory be—
There's a power of terrible things you'd see
    In the dark.

BLACKBERRY TIME

In blackberry time herself and me
  We do be up by break of day ;
An' " God go with us now," says she,
  " The time we're thravellin' on our way
An' God go with us all the while
We're thravellin' on from mile to mile."

'Tis up Glencullen way we are—
  The berries there is fine and sweet ;
But kilt you'd be, it is so far,
  When you go thravellin' on your feet.
Och ! weary miles ere you'd come down
From far Glencullen to the town.

Up there at dawn 'tis quare and still,
  And dew lies heavy on the ground.
But berries for a basket's fill
  Grows on the bushes all around.

And whiles we'll rest and eat a few
That's sodden wid the heavy dew.

We traipis round from door to door,
  'Tis weary in the noonday heat.
(May God have mercy on the poor
  That thravels round upon their feet!)
For sure you're moidhered in the town,
The way the carts go up an' down.

But when we're quit of all our load,
  "Now God be praised for that," says she ;
And back we go the homeward road,
  Near bet we are herself and me.
Och ! sure the thought of home is sweet
To thim that thravels on their feet.

THE WEST WIND

Last night the air was cold and still,
No breeze was moving in Glendhu;
The golden beech leaves scarcely stirred
Above my head as I went through.
From every cottage rose the smoke,
An' not a breath its column broke.
Brown in the glen the bracken grew,
No broken leaf or stem you'd find.
But after dawn the gale awoke,
The world seemed rocking in the wind.

Across the Wicklow hills he came,
The herdsmen felt his great wings beat;
The waves of Lough Nahanagan
Were ruffled by his flying feet;
The Vale of Clara felt him pass
Swift-foot across the meadow grass;

They heard him where the waters meet,
He made the pines and larches sway;
He crossed the stream at Glenmacnass,
And blew the falls to silver spray.

They heard his pipes in Glenmalure,
He sang a song of Western seas;
The withered leaves in Glendalough
Rose up and rustled round his knees;
He shook the beeches of Glendhu
To golden rain as he passed through.
He bent Glencullen's tallest trees,
His breath was rough on bird and beast,
Across the mountain tops he flew
To take his pleasure in the east.

Oh, wild wind from the distant west,
Be still again and give us rest.

SONGS IN THREE COUNTIES

SAYS SHE

My Granny she often says to me,
Says she, " You're terrible bold,
It's you have a right to mend your ways
Before you'll ever grow old,"
       Says she.
" Before you'll ever grow old.
For it's steadfast now that you ought to be,
An' you going on sixteen," says she.
" What'll you do when you're old like me ?
What'll you do ? " says she.

" What will I do when I'm old ?" says I.
" Och Musha, I'll say my prayers,
I'll wear a net an' a black lace cap
To cover my silver hairs,"
      Says I.
" To cover my silver hairs.

When I am as old as Kate Kearney's cat
I'll sell my dress and featherdy hat,
An' buy an old bedgown the like o' that,
The very like o' that."

My Granny she sighs and says to me,
" The years fly terrible fast,
The girls they laugh an' talk with the boys,
But they all grow old at last,"
      Says she.
" They all grow old at last.
At Epiphany cocks may skip," says she,
" But kilt by Easter they're like to be.
By the Hokey ! you'll grow as old as me,
As weak an' old," says she.

" Maybe you tell me no lie," says I,
" But I've time before me yet.
There's time to dance and there's time to sing,
So why would I need to fret ? "
      Says I.
" So why would I need to fret ?

Old age may lie at the foot of the hill,
'Twixt hoppin' and trottin' we'll get there still.
Why wouldn't we dance while we have the will,
Dance while we have the will?"

EASTER SNOW

(Written to the tune "Easter Snow," in Miss Honoria Gal-
wey's Collection of Irish Airs   When the blackthorn blossoms
are falling the country people call it Easter snow.)

My jewel of the world, she sleeps so fast,
  She will not hear you, Spring wind, if you blow ;
So let you shake the blossoms of the thorn
  Till her bed is hidden deep in Easter snow.

Bright jewel of my heart, she sleeps at last,
  O kind Earth, wrap her round in your brown shawl.
Sing soft to her and rock her in your arms
  So she'll not be lonesome after me at all.

I hear the childher laugh as they run past,
  They see their mother watching at the door ;
It's long I'll wait beside the lonely hearth,
  For there's sorra child of mine will cross the floor

EASTER SNOW

O thorn trees round her grave, now let you cast
  Your snow upon the place she takes her rest.
The while I stay and cheat my heart with dreams
  That I'm holding her again upon my breast.

BOYS

I do be thinking God must laugh
The time He makes a boy ;
All element the creatures are,
And divilmint and joy.
Careless and gay as a wad in a window,*
Swift as a redshanks, and wild as a hare ;
Heartscalds and torments—but sorra a mother
Has got one to spare.

* "Wad in a window." The bunch of rags so often seen
fluttering from the broken windows of an Irish cabin ; hence the
frequent use of this comparison.

MY BLESSING BE ON WATERFORD

My blessing be on Waterford, the town of ships,
  For it's what I love to be streeling on the quay,
Watching while the boats go out, watching them
    come in,
    And thinking of a one I know that's sailing far
    away.

It's well to be in Waterford, to see the ships,
  The great big masts of them against the evening
    sky,
Seagulls flying round, and the men unloading them,
  With quare strange talk among themselves the
    time you're passing by.

I love to be in Waterford, to see the ships come in,
  Bringing in their cargoes from west, and east, and
    south.
Some day one I love will stand here upon the quay,
  He'll take my two hands in his own, and stoop to
    kiss my mouth.

THIEF OF THE WORLD

Oh, it's little Rosanne is the rogue of the world !
  If it's villany in it,
    Herself will be there,
  An' it's like she'll begin it
    With time an' to spare.
For she's pullin' my coat,
Or she's teasing the goat,
Or huntin' the chuckins,
The little old dote.
Or maybe she's off on her two little toes,
An' the Mischief is puzzled to guess where she goes.

Oh, it's little Rosanne is the thief of the world !
  If you're hearin' her laughter,
    You'd best be aware,
  For there's something she's after,
    But who can tell where ?

For she's lookin' for eggs,
Or the basket of pegs,
Or she's chasin' the ducks
Till they're run off their legs.
There's nothin' that's safe! I've a right now to
    know,—
For she's stolen my heart on me three years ago.

THE KERRY COW

It's in Connacht or in Munster that yourself might
  travel wide,
And be asking all the herds you'd meet along the
  country-side,
But you'd never meet a one could show the likes of
  her till now,
Where she's grazing in a Leinster field—my little
  Kerry cow.

If herself went to the cattle fairs she'd put all cows
  to shame,
For the finest poets of the land would meet to sing
  her fame;
And the young girls would be asking leave to stroke
  her satin coat,
They'd be praising and caressing her, and calling
  her a dote.

If the King of Spain gets news of her he'll fill his
    purse with gold,
And set sail to ask the English King where she is to
    be sold.
But the King of Spain may come to me, a crown
    upon his brow.
It is he may keep his golden purse—and I my Kerry
    cow.

The priest maybe will tell her fame to the Holy
    Pope of Rome,
And the Cardinals' College send for her to leave her
    Irish home;
But it's heart-broke she would be itself to cross the
    Irish sea,
'Twould be best they'd send a blessing to my Kerry
    cow and me.

When the Ulster men hear tell of her, they'll come
    with swords an' pikes,
For it's civil war there'll be no less if they should see
    her likes,

And you'll read it on the paper of the bloody fight
    there's been,
An' the Orangemen they're burying in fields of
    Leinster green.

There are red cows that's contrary, and there's white
    cows quare and wild,
But my Kerry cow is biddable, an' gentle as a child.
You may rare up kings and heroes on the lovely
    milk she yields,
For she's fit to foster generals to fight our battlefields.

In the histories they'll be making they've a right to
    put her name
With the horse of Troy and Oisin's hounds and other
    beasts of fame.
And the painters will be painting her beneath the
    hawthorn bough
Where she's grazing on the good green grass—my
    little Kerry cow.

SPRING, THE TRAVELLING MAN

SPRING, the Travelling Man, has been here,
    Here in the glen;
He must have passed by in the grey of the dawn,
    When only the robin and wren
    Were awake,
Watching out with their bright little eyes
    In the midst of the brake.
    The rabbits, maybe, heard him pass,
    Stepping light on the grass,
Whistling careless and gay at the break o' the day.
    Then the blackthorn to give him delight
    Put on raiment of white:
    And all for his sake.
    The gorse on the hill, where he rested an hour,
    Grew bright with a splendour of flower.
    My grief! that I was not aware
    Of himself being there;

It is I would have given my dower
To have seen him set forth,
Whistling careless and gay in the grey of the morn,
By gorse bush and fraughan and thorn,
On his way to the north.

THE RICH WOMAN

Hay in the haggard, and cows in the byre,
A turf stack is filled with its store for the fire.
What way am I wanting my heart's deep desire?

Linen new woven and meal in the chest,
A cloak of red frieze that I bought in the west:
But sorra a babe I can rock on my breast.

Money laid by and a parcel of land,
A boat in the harbour, the house where I stand—
But God! for a child that would clutch at my hand.

Milk and fresh butter and flour to spare,
The chuckins, the goats, an' the turkeys to rare:
But never a little wee child I can care.

The beggar goes by, a babe in her shawl,
A wee one streels after and runs at her call.
'Tis I am the beggar, and she that has all.

God send me a child with the sorrow and pain,
Let him waken the quiet and squander the gain,
For I'm counting my riches and plenty in vain.

A child that will know to spoil and to tear,
What matter the trouble and moidher and care,
So I'm hearing the fall of his feet on the stair?

A beggar I am—shall I not be blessed
With a baby come home that will sleep on my breast?
Let me be a mother, O Christ, with the rest!

GLORNY'S WEIR

At night when the world was sleepy and still,
I'd wake, maybe, in the depth o' the dark,
And think of the river below the hill,
That flows so fast by the ruined old mill.
Never a sound beside would I hear,
But the water roaring at Glorny's Weir.

I'd think to myself how day would come soon,
The water-hens wake, and the wagtails stir,
The kingfisher flash in the light of the noon
From the willowy banks of Knockmaroon.
But through the day you could scarcely hear
The voice of the river at Glorny's Weir.

I'd wake in the depth o' the dark, maybe,
When the friendly voices of day were still;

But the river would lift its song for me,
Down from the mountains off to the sea.
And glad was I in the night to hear
The roar of the waters at Glorny's Weir.

IRISH SKIES

In London here the streets are grey, an' grey the sky
    above ;
I wish I were in Ireland to see the skies I love—
Pearl cloud, buff cloud, the colour of a dove.

All day I travel English streets, but in my dreams I
    tread
The far Glencullen road and see the soft sky over-
    head,
Grey clouds, white clouds, the wind has shepherded.

At night the London lamps shine bright, but what
    are they to me ?
I've seen the moonlight in Glendhu, the stars above
    Glenchree—
The lamps of Heav'n give light enough for me.

The city in the winter time put on a shroud of
    smoke,
But the sky above the Three rock was blue as Mary's
    cloak,
Ruffled like doves' wings when the wind awoke.

I dream I see the Wicklow hills by evening sunlight
    kissed,
An' every glen and valley there brimful of radiant
    mist—
The jewelled sky topaz and amethyst.

I wake to see the London streets, the sombre sky
    above,
God's blessing on the far-off roads, and on the skies I
    love,—
Pearl feather, grey feather, wings of a dove.

THE KIND COMPANION

I lost my kind companion this Friday was a week,
The likes of him, my decent man, you might go far
    to seek.
       'Tis woeful now, my comrade gone,
         To be so sad and lone,
     ' Myself upon the green earth still,
         An' him beneath a stone.

A quiet man he always was, and quietly he died,
With ne'er a word and ne'er a call to bring me to his
    side.
       My grief, my grief! the way I am
         To sit here lone and sad,
       An' never see himself, or hear
         The kindly word he had.

Ah! whisper, honey, quare old ways I have for lettin'
    on
That he's still in it all the time I know his body's
    gone.

For sometimes when I wet the tay,
    I do be talking fast,
Pretending all the whiles himself
    Will answer me at last.

An' sometimes, sitting by the fire, I think I hear his
    tread,
" 'Tis sure himself," I say those times, " that's stirrin'
    overhead."
        'Tis only notions that I have
          That do divert my mind,
        When waiting here in lonesomeness
          I hear the rising wind.

'Tis closing in on fifty year since him and me got
    wed,
A quiet man he always was, an' few the words he
    said ;
        But sure he had a right itself
          To take me with him too.
        My quiet kind companion,
          That God may welcome you !

SONG

If you let Sorrow in on you,
    Surely she'll stay,
Sitting there by the hearth
    Till you wish her away.

If you see the grey cloak of her
    Down the boreen,
Let you close the door softly
    And wait there unseen.

For if she comes in on you
    Never you'll part,
Till the fire burns out
    In the core of your heart.

DREAMS

My son is in America
  Away beyond the sea,
But in his dreams he comes back home,
  And looks out towards Knockiee.
He sees the ribbon of white road
  Go winding towards Glenchree,
And he knocks with his stick on the open door
  To call herself and me.

All day he's working in the town,
  And moidhered with the street,
But in his dreams he feels the grass—
  The grass beneath his feet.
He wanders up the green hill-side,
  The elder bloom smells sweet,
Then he praises God for the Irish air
  And reek of burning peat.

The wonders of the West he sees,
    For men of wealth live there
In houses reaching to the stars,
    With everything that's fair.
" But oh ! " says he, " the hills for me,
    The sight of grouse or hare,
The cry of the curlews over the bog,
    The breath of Irish air."

BLESSINGS

It's what I thank God for each night,
A little cabin that's mine by right,
The strength of a man for work or fight,
    And food and light.

It's what I thank God for each day—
A wife with never too much to say,
A wife, a dog, and a child for play,
    For those I'd pray.

I thank God for the land I tread,
A pipe to smoke and an easy bed,
The thatch I made that's over my head,
    And daily bread.

I thank God for an Irish name,
And a son of mine to bear the same,
My own to love me and none to blame:
    No more I'd claim.

SCHOLARS

Iᴛ is pity I have,
  And that is a truth,
For the Trinity men
  And the men of Maynooth.
The men of Maynooth are the like o' the rooks,
With their solemn black coats an' their serious
  looks.
An' the Trinity men are no better at all,
For when they're not studyin' deep in their books
Their only diversion is batting a ball,
  An' that is a truth.

If myself now were there
  My heart would be broke,
For the smell o' the earth
  Or a whiff of peat smoke.
The weight of their learning would sure have me
  bet,
I'd sell all their books for an old fishing net,

And pawn their professors for Danny's young horse.
Now glory to goodness, I'd pine and I'd fret
For the mountainy wind an' the smell o' the gorse,
    An' that is a truth.

    It's the old ones that's there,
      They'd ask a poor lad
    To be searching his mind
      For what knowledge he had.
For learning in poaching they'd give me small
    thanks,
Or for tricks to catch trout hidden under the banks.
There's much I could tell them of grouse and of
    hare,
But still they'd not bid me to enter their ranks,
An' faith ! I'm not wishful to be with them there,
    An' that is a truth.

PRAYER FOR A LITTLE CHILD

God keep my jewel this day from danger ;
From tinker and pooka and black-hearted stranger.
From harm of the water, from hurt of the fire.
From the horns of the cows going home to the byre.
From sight of the fairies that maybe might change
    her.
From teasing the ass when he's tied to the manger.
From stones that would bruise her, from thorns of
    the briar.
From red evil berries that wake her desire.
From hunting the gander and vexing the goat.
From the depths o' sea water by Danny's old boat.
From cut and from tumble, from sickness and weep-
    ing ;
May God have my jewel this day in His keeping.

TIM, AN IRISH TERRIER

It's wonderful dogs they're breeding now :
Small as a flea or large as a cow
But my old lad Tim he'll never be bet
By any dog that ever he met.
"Come on," says he, " for I'm not kilt yet."

No matter the size of the dog he'll meet,
Tim trails his coat the length o' the street.
D'ye mind his scars an' his ragged ear,
The like of a Dublin Fusilier ?
He's a massacree dog that knows no fear.

But he'd stick to me till his latest breath :
An' he'd go with me to the gates of death.
He'd wait for a thousand years, maybe,
Scratching the door an' whining for me
If myself were inside in Purgatary.

So I laugh when I hear thim make it plain
That dogs and men never meet again.
For all their talk who'd listen to thim,
With the soul in the shining eyes of him?
Would God be wasting a dog like Tim?

TO C. L. G., IN GRATITUDE

THE blessings of blessings for him
That has always time to be kind,
A blessing running before,
A blessing trottin' behind ;
An angel caring his house
To drive away every sorrow ;
Good luck at his heels to-day,
Good luck on his path to-morrow.
A place for him up in Heav'n,
And St. Peter there at the gate
With the kindly welcome word
And himself not bid to wait :
For I'm thinking the saint will say,
" Come in here out of the wind,
It's not so often I see
A man that has time to be kind.

A SOFT DAY

A soft day, thank God!
A wind from the south
With a honeyed mouth;
A scent of drenching leaves.
' Briar and beech and lime,
White elder-flower and thyme
And the soaking grass smells sweet,
Crushed by my two bare feet,
While the rain drips,
Drips, drips, drips from the eaves.

A soft day, thank God!
The hills wear a shroud
Of silver cloud;
The web the spider weaves
Is a glittering net;
The woodland path is wet,

And the soaking earth smells sweet
Under my two bare feet,
   And the rain drips,
Drips, drips, drips from the leaves.

I

THE CHRISTMAS GUEST

If Mary came to the door to-night,
In the bitter wind and soaking rain ;
If she came to me in her sorry plight,
To plead as one woman pleads with another,
As mothers come in their need to a mother,
If Mary came in the wind and rain,
She never should beg at my door in vain.

If Mary came to the door to-night,
Her Baby sleeping upon her breast,
Saying, " Let you share with me warmth and light,
For I bear in my arms the World's Desire,
But cold are His limbs, and we have no fire ;
O stranger woman, may you be blessed,
If you open your door and give us rest."

If Mary stood and knocked at my door,
A thousand welcomes herself should find ;

And she'd not be scorning a house so poor,
With the homespun linen upon the table:
No place she found one time but a stable—
With the poor dumb beasts were good and kind—
And a thatch to shield her from rain and wind.

If Mary came, the Mother of God,
The Rose of the World upon her breast;
Oh ! I'd sweep the ashes, and turn the sod,
And bring her new bread and cakes of my baking,
With the freshest butter, this morning's making.
Happy the home could offer rest
To the new-born Child, earth's Christmas Guest.

PRINTED BY WILLIAM CLOWES AND SONS, LIMITED, LONDON AND BECCLES, ENGLAND